Navigate the Emerald Coast

Sponsors

BEEF JERKY OUTLET

Destin Commons
4311 Legendary Drive, #133D
Destin, Florida 32541
(850) 460-2336

CARPET CITY

2 Eglin Parkway South
Fort Walton Beach, Florida 32548
(850) 244-1161

DESIGNS & ACCESSORIES

246 Eglin Parkway Northeast
Fort Walton Beach, Florida 32547
(850) 651-3324

FACTORY DIRECT FURNITURE DESTIN

331 Harbor Boulevard
Destin, Florida 32541
(850) 502-5896

FURNITURE RESOURCES

425 Mary Esther Cut Off Northwest
Fort Walton Beach, Florida 32548
(850) 243-3533

GEORGE'S AT ALYS BEACH

30 Castle Harbour Drive
Alys Beach, Florida 32461
(850) 641-0017

MAGNOLIA GRILL

157 Brooks Street Southeast
Fort Walton Beach, Florida 32548
(850) 302-0266

Welcome to Paradise

Whether you're a lifelong resident or a first-time visitor, there's always something new to discover about the Emerald Coast. But let's face it, the hook here is our beaches, which continually are recognized among the world's finest.

The sun. The surf. The sugar-white sand (you won't burn your feet here). The Gulf of Mexico providing a shimmering turquoise backdrop and spectacular sunsets.

It's why millions of visitors return to our neck of the woods every year.

Simply, welcome to paradise.

Navigate the Emerald Coast is a reader's guide to our beaches. Across Santa Rosa, Okaloosa, and Walton counties, there are thirty distinct beach destinations and beach communities to explore. A few are private locations with limited public access, but most come free of charge. Think of them as rooms with amazing views that last a lifetime.

Inside the following pages, you'll learn about each of the beach destinations stretched across more than sixty miles of our coastline. Along the journey, you'll even pick up a few recipes from chefs who serve fresh seafood cuisine at our most popular eateries.

So this book is about our coast. Well, your coast.

Enjoy!

Table of Contents

BEACHES OF SOUTH WALTON
6

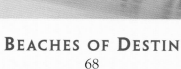

Beaches of South Walton

Alys Beach

One might get the sense they're not on Scenic Highway 30A anymore when passing by Alys Beach.
The stark, white architecture and the perfect rows of palm trees present a modern seaside community
that features everything you'd dream of for a vacation destination.

THE LOWDOWN
Make the time to walk around the community and take advantage of the parks and spacious green areas. Ever wonder why everything is a uniform white? Not only is it a good photo-op, but also it keeps the buildings cooler. When you're there, stroll along the nature trail or bike along the streets.

WHAT'S NEARBY
George's at Alys Beach, 30 Castle Harbour Drive (American); Caliza Restaurant, 23 Nonesuch Way (contemporary American); Fonville Press, 147 West La Garza Lane (coffee, pastries, wine).

BEST BEACH . . .
photos. The architecture is the perfect backdrop for an Instagram.

BEACH ACCESS
Private, but you can check out the views from Gulf Green.

CIRCA 2008

GEORGE'S
AT ALYS BEACH

George's at Alys Beach

Watermelon Tuna Poke

MISO GINGER VINAIGRETTE

1/2	cup white miso		1	cup water
3	ounces ginger, peeled		1	tablespoon chili garlic sauce (sambal)
1	shallot		1	tablespoon salt
1/2	cup rice wine vinegar		2	cups canola oil or vegetable oil

POKE

4	ounces yellowtail tuna, finely diced			Canola oil or vegetable oil
4	ounces watermelon, finely diced			Salt to taste
1	plantain, thinly sliced		1	avocado, sliced (optional)

For the Miso Ginger Vinaigrette, combine the miso, ginger, shallot, vinegar, water, chili garlic sauce and salt in a blender and process until smooth. Add the canola oil gradually, processing constantly until smooth.

For the Poke, combine the tuna, watermelon and about 1 ounce of the Miso Ginger Vinaigrette in a bowl and toss gently to mix.

Fry the plantain in a small amount of canola oil in a skillet until crispy. Remove to paper towels to drain. Season with salt.

To plate, spoon a portion of the Poke onto a salad plate. Add fried plantain and avocado slices. Serve immediately.

Yield: 2 or 3 servings

CHEF CAMILLE WITHALL

Blue Mountain Beach

Known for its blue lupine flowers (hence the name), Blue Mountain is a cozy spot on Scenic Highway 30A, representing both old Florida and new with beach cottages and luxurious mansions.
The spot was "established" in 1948, according to the painted sign at the beach.
Grab an ice cream cone at Blue Mountain Beach Creamery and take a trip back in time.

THE LOWDOWN   Blue Mountain is a mix of locals and visitors and is tucked away from most of the hustle and bustle found in the beach communities popular to tourists. You'll likely still have traffic problems in the summer, but there's plenty to occupy your time while you wait.

WHAT'S NEARBY   Basmati's, 3295 Scenic Highway 30A (Asian cuisine); Marie's Bistro, 2260 Scenic Highway 30A (sushi); Grecian Gardens, 3375 Scenic Highway 30A (Greek cuisine); Blue Mountain Beach Creamery, 2129 South County Highway 83 (ice cream).

BEST BEACH ...   sign. The old white and blue sign welcoming you to Blue Mountain Beach has a vintage feel to it. The sign depicts the blue lupines and clearly states "local traffic only."

BEACH ACCESS   Blue Mountain Regional Beach Access, 2365 South County Highway 83.

OTHER ACCESS   Blue Lake Road Neighborhood Access, 726 Blue Mountain Road. Walk-up traffic only.

BASMATI'S ASIAN CUISINE

Chocolate Tofu Pie

3	cups crushed Oreos
4	tablespoons butter, melted
14	ounces semisweet chocolate
1/4	cup light corn syrup
12	ounces firm silken tofu
12	ounces soft silken tofu

Process the Oreos in a food processor until finely ground. Add the butter and process until all of the crumbs are coated. Press the mixture over the bottom of a springform pan.

Melt the chocolate in a glass bowl in the microwave, stirring frequently to prevent burning. Stir in the corn syrup.

Blend the firm tofu and soft tofu in a food processor until smooth. Add the chocolate mixture and blend until creamy and fully incorporated. Pour over the Oreo crust and smooth the top. Chill for at least 6 hours. Run a sharp knife around the edge of the pie and remove the side of the pan.

Yield: 8 to 10 servings

CHEF TEAM NATTAKIT LAMMA, WERAPON POONSAWAT, NATE LINCK, AND CARLOS MENDOZA

Dune Allen

Like the beach? Like the coastal dune lakes?
You can get the best of both worlds in the Dune Allen beach neighborhood.
Bring your bike, pack a picnic, and explore the area.

THE LOWDOWN   Three of the coastal dune lakes are within the Dune Allen beach neighborhood (Stallworth, Allen, and Oyster lakes). Bike along the Timpoochee Trail, do a little fishing (you can get supplies at Stinky's Bait Shack), and be sure to make a stop on the Oyster Lake Bridge and look around.

WHAT'S NEARBY   Stinky's Fish Camp, 5994 West Scenic Highway 30A (seafood); Vue on 30A, 4801 West Scenic Highway 30A (new American); Elmo's Grill, 6931 West Scenic Highway 30A (seafood).

BEST BEACH . . .   for multitasking. See the lakes, the beach, and enjoy nature.

BEACH ACCESS   5753 West Scenic Highway 30A.

STINKY'S
FISH CAMP

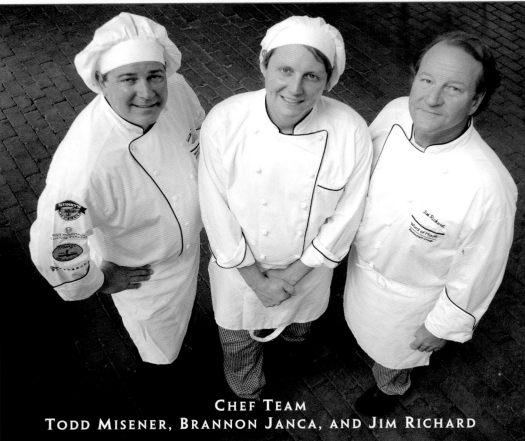

CHEF TEAM
TODD MISENER, BRANNON JANCA, AND JIM RICHARD

Unca Duke's Barbecue Shrimp

SAUCE BASE

$^1/4$ cup Unca Duke's Geaux Jus Premium Pepper Sauce	$^1/4$ cup Worcestershire sauce	$^1/4$ cup shrimp stock
	$^1/4$ cup white wine	$1^1/4$ tablespoons Crystal hot sauce

SHRIMP

5 (16/20) shrimp	2 lemons, sliced	1 tablespoon chopped green onions
Salt and pepper to taste	$1^1/2$ teaspoons cracked black pepper	1 tablespoon chopped fresh parsley
1 tablespoon vegetable oil	6 tablespoons butter	1 (3-inch) slice of garlic bread, toasted

For the Sauce Base, combine the Geaux Jus, Worcestershire sauce, wine, shrimp stock and hot sauce in a bowl and mix well.

For the Shrimp, heat a sauté pan briefly over medium heat. Season the shrimp with salt and pepper. Combine the shrimp, vegetable oil, lemon slices and cracked black pepper in the sauté pan. Sauté until the shrimp are half cooked. Deglaze the pan with the Sauce Base. Cook until the sauce is reduced by half, stirring occasionally. Add the butter in small pieces. Cook until the butter is partially melted, shaking the pan vigorously. Add the green onions and shake the pan. Cook until the butter is melted. Add the parsley and shake the pan.

To plate, place the garlic bread in the center of a plate. Spoon the shrimp mixture around the bread.

Yield: 1 serving

Grayton Beach

Alongside towering condominiums and Gulf-front homes sits Grayton Beach State Park, where you can camp or just head to the beach for the day. The best part is that admission to get in costs less than that fancy drink you enjoyed down the road.

THE LOWDOWN   Anytime you can enjoy the beach at a state park, you should go for it. There's not a huge walk from the parking lot to the beach. It's clean, and you can enjoy an untouched shore. There are also hiking trails, a boat ramp, and fishing spots. And if you want to stay overnight, cabins are $130 a night during peak season (February 1 to July 31). Entrance fees are $2-$5. You can also check out Western Lake, which is part of the park.

WHAT'S NEARBY   Chiringo, 63 Hotz Avenue (local seafood, tapas, Spanish-inspired dishes); The Red Bar, 70 Hotz Avenue (southern fare); Pandora's, 63 Defuniak Street (steakhouse); Hurricane Oyster Bar & Grill, 37 Logan Lane #4 (seafood shack).

BEST BEACH . . .   to enjoy nature. You're not just at the beach, you're located near untouched nature, such as coastal dune lakes, wet flatwoods, and estuarine marshes. You can explore more of the area's natural beauty at Grayton Beach State Park.

BEACH ACCESS   357 Main Park Road, Santa Rosa Beach.

OTHER ACCESS   Grayton Dunes Access, located at the end of Garfield Street behind The Red Bar. ADA-accessible, parking, and showers.

Roasted Mahi

At Chiringo, we marinade mahi in canning jars and serve it with caper berries, house-pickled veggies, and lahvosh.

ESCABECHE MARINADE

1 tablespoon olive oil	1 teaspoon chopped fresh thyme
2 ribs celery, finely chopped	2 teaspoons salt
1/2 red onion, finely chopped	2 teaspoons sugar
1/4 red bell pepper, finely chopped	1 cup white vinegar
1 jalapeño pepper, finely chopped	1/4 cup olive oil
1 (2-ounce) carrot, finely chopped	Juice of 1 lemon
3 garlic cloves, chopped	1/4 cup sliced kalamata olives
2 tablespoons chopped fresh parsley	2 tablespoons capers
1 teaspoon dried oregano	

For the Escabeche Marinade, heat 1 tablespoon olive oil over medium heat in a sauté pan. Add the celery, onion, bell pepper, jalapeño pepper, carrot and garlic to the oil and sweat for 5 minutes or until tender.

Combine the parsley, oregano, thyme, salt, sugar and vinegar in a food processor. Add 1/4 cup olive oil gradually, processing constantly to make a vinaigrette.

Combine the sautéed vegetables, vinaigrette, lemon juice, olives and capers in a bowl and mix well.

Note: This marinade can be used with any flaky fish or shellfish and is great with octopus. One of our family favorites is Ensalada de Pulpo, which is cooked octopus that has been marinated with the Escabeche Marinade and is served with tomato, avocado, and boiled green banana.

MAHI

2	pounds mahi
1	tablespoon olive oil
1	teaspoon salt
1	teaspoon cracked pepper

For the Mahi, preheat the oven to 325 degrees. Rub both sides of the mahi with the olive oil and season with the salt and pepper. Place the fish on a baking sheet. Bake for 25 minutes. Let stand to cool. Remove the mahi to a bowl and use hands to flake the fish.

Pour the Escabeche Marinade over the Mahi and stir gently using a spatula.

Yield: 15 or 16 servings

CHIRINGO

Gulf Place

Gulf Place is a small nook within Scenic Highway 30A but has more to offer than meets the eye.
Of course, a perfect public access spot is key,
but there's also plenty to do when the sun goes down.

THE LOWDOWN   Right across from Ed Walline Park is the Gulf Place Town Center, where you can eat, drink, and shop, and no one will judge you for your sandy feet. You can also take a stroll or bike along Timpoochee Trail. Don't want to get sandy? The park's boardwalk has a good observation deck so you can get your sunset photo.

WHAT'S NEARBY   The Perfect Pig, 7 Town Center Loop (upscale southern comfort food); Pizza by the Sea, 95 Laura Hamilton Boulevard (pizza, fresh Italian); Goatfeathers, 3865 West Scenic Highway 30A (American, seafood).

BEST BEACH . . .   to "forget" to pack your lunch. The stuff you really want to indulge in is right across the street.

BEACH ACCESS   Ed Walline Park, 4447 West Scenic Highway 30A.

Bacon-Wrapped Jumbo Scallops

Bacon-Wrapped Scallops topped with crumbled goat cheese and prosciutto over Parmesan-Crusted Fingerling Potatoes with Wilted Spinach and Tomatoes.

PARMESAN-CRUSTED FINGERLING POTATOES

5	fingerling potatoes		Salt and pepper to taste
	Vegetable oil		Shredded Parmesan cheese
1	tablespoon butter		Chopped fresh parsley
1	garlic clove, minced		

WILTED SPINACH AND TOMATOES

2	ounces tomatoes, chopped	2	cups packed spinach
1	garlic clove, minced	1/16	teaspoon salt
1	tablespoon olive oil		

SCALLOPS

4	slices of bacon		Salt and pepper to taste
4	jumbo scallops	1	ounce goat cheese, crumbled
4	(4-inch) skewers	4	ounces prosciutto, sliced

For the Parmesan-Crusted Fingerling Potatoes, combine the potatoes and enough water to cover in a saucepan. Bring to a boil over high heat. Cook for 25 to 30 minutes or until a knife cuts through the potatoes easily; drain.

Coat the bottom of a skillet with vegetable oil. Cut the potatoes lengthwise into halves and arrange skin side up in the skillet. Cook over medium-high heat until the bottoms of the potatoes are golden brown. Loosen the potatoes using a spatula. Add the butter, garlic, salt and pepper and mix well. Drain off any excess butter. Sprinkle with Parmesan cheese and parsley.

For the Wilted Spinach and Tomatoes, sauté the tomatoes and garlic in the olive oil in a skillet until the garlic starts to brown. Add the spinach and salt and toss to mix well.

For the Scallops, preheat the oven to 400 degrees.

Cook the bacon in a cast-iron skillet or heavy ovenproof skillet over very low heat just until partially cooked. Remove to paper towels, reserving the drippings in the skillet.

Wrap a slice of bacon around each scallop, securing the bacon with a skewer. Season both sides with salt and pepper. Sear the scallops on both sides in the reserved bacon drippings. Bake for 5 to 8 minutes or until cooked through.

To plate, spoon the Parmesan-Crusted Fingerling Potatoes onto the center of a serving plate. Plate the Wilted Spinach and Tomatoes. Arrange the Scallops on top of the potatoes, carefully removing the skewers. Top each scallop with a fourth of the goat cheese and 1 ounce of prosciutto. Garnish the plate with chopped fresh parsley.

Yield: 1 serving

CHEF JOSH BRUNKEN

Inlet Beach

*At the very end (or beginning) of South Walton is Inlet Beach,
the largest public beach access of the county's sixteen coastal communities.
Largely untouched, Inlet Beach is a good pick for nature lovers or big groups
who don't want to fight for space on the beach.*

THE LOWDOWN   When you want to explore the area, you can choose between heading west on Scenic Highway 30A to Rosemary Beach or venturing farther into Panama City. If you want a laid-back beach day, Inlet Beach might be a long drive for some, but it's worth it.

WHAT'S NEARBY   Cuvee 30A, 12805 Highway 98 East, Suite D101 (fine dining, featuring fresh Gulf seafood); Shades Bar & Grill, 10952 East Scenic Highway 30A (pizza, wings); Donut Hole Inlet Beach, 75 North Wall Street (American breakfast).

BEST BEACH . . .   to sneak over to Rosemary Beach. Just kidding. However, if you have the stamina, you can essentially walk over to the private Rosemary Beach access. The shoreline is public property.

BEACH ACCESS   At the end of South Orange Street, about 100 yards south of U.S. Highway 98.

Eggplant Medallions with Jumbo Lump Crabmeat

HOLLANDAISE SAUCE
1/2 cup (1 stick) butter, cut into
    small pieces
2 egg yolks
1 tablespoon lemon juice
1/8 teaspoon Tabasco sauce
1/4 cup white wine
2 teaspoons vanilla extract

MEUNIÈRE SAUCE
1/2 cup veal demi-glace
1/2 cup white wine
2 tablespoons lemon juice
1/2 cup (1 stick) butter, cut into
    small pieces

EGGPLANT MEDALLIONS
Canola oil for frying
1/2 cup milk
1/4 cup Chef Tim Creehan's Grill Plus
    All Purpose Seasoning
1 eggplant, peeled and sliced
2 cups corn flour

SAUTÉED LUMP CRABMEAT
2 tablespoons butter
8 ounces jumbo lump crabmeat
1 green onion, chopped
2 teaspoons lemon juice
Salt and white pepper to taste

SAUCE DESIGN
2 tablespoons heavy cream
2 tablespoons sour cream

12 (3-inch) chive stems

For the Hollandaise Sauce, melt the butter in a saucepan over low heat. Let stand to cool completely. Blend the egg yolks, lemon juice and Tabasco sauce in the metal bowl of a double boiler. Heat the wine and vanilla extract in a small saucepan over low heat; flambé. Add the wine mixture gradually to the egg yolk mixture, whisking constantly to blend. Cook over a double boiler, whisking constantly until firm peaks form. Remove from the heat. Whisk in the melted butter. Keep warm.

CHEF TIM CREEHAN

For the Meunière Sauce, combine the demi-glace, wine and lemon juice in a saucepan and mix well. Cook until reduced by half, stirring frequently. Remove from the heat. Add the butter a piece at a time, whisking until smooth after each addition. Keep warm.

30

For the Eggplant Medallions, heat the canola oil to 350 degrees in a deep fryer or electric skillet. Mix the milk and Grill Plus in a bowl. Dip the eggplant into the milk mixture and coat with the corn flour. Fry in the hot oil until golden brown; remove to paper towels to drain.

For the Sautéed Lump Crabmeat, melt the butter in a sauté pan over medium heat. Add the crabmeat, green onion, lemon juice, salt and white pepper. Cook until heated through, stirring carefully.

For the Sauce Design, combine the heavy cream and sour cream in a bowl and mix well. Pour into a squeeze bottle.

To plate, spoon a fourth of the Meunière Sauce onto a plate and decorate with a fourth of the Sauce Design. Arrange a portion of the Eggplant Medallions in the center of the plate and top with a portion of the Sautéed Lump Crabmeat. Drizzle with Hollandaise Sauce. Place 3 chive stems on top of the crabmeat.

Yield: 4 servings

CUVEE 30A

Miramar Beach

Miramar Beach is more than a Spring Break hot spot. In fact, it's a good place for groups of friends and families who want to just walk over to the beach. Even if you're just strolling along Scenic Highway 98, you can still get a glimpse of the Gulf.

THE LOWDOWN While cars are rushing down U.S. Highway 98, Scenic Highway 98 is like a parallel universe, where you can bike, walk, or jog at your leisure along the road. There's plenty of dining along the scenic road and even more options when you venture onto the main 98. And if you like shopping, there's plenty of it at Silver Sands Premium Outlets.

WHAT'S NEARBY Pompano Joe's, 2237 Scenic Gulf Drive (Caribbean, seafood); Dynasty Chinese Cuisine, 12889 U.S. Highway 98 West (Chinese); Capt. Dave's on the Gulf, 3796 Scenic Highway 98 (American, seafood).

BEST BEACH . . . to go for a walk. You can technically walk the beach without trudging through the sand by strolling down the walkway.

BEACH ACCESS Miramar Beach Regional Beach Access, 2375 Scenic Highway 98.

POMPANO JOE'S SEAFOOD HOUSE

Montego Bay Tuna

Pan-seared jerk-style tuna served with a tropical fresh fruit salsa.

FRESH FRUIT SALSA

3   ounces pineapple (about 1 slice),
    peeled and finely chopped
3   ounces mango (about 1/2 mango),
    peeled and finely chopped
3   ounces papaya (about 1 wedge),
    peeled, seeded and finely chopped
1   jalapeño pepper, finely chopped
    (optional)
1   teaspoon fresh lime juice
1   teaspoon salt

TUNA

1   (14-ounce) tuna, cut into 2 steaks
1   tablespoon extra-virgin olive oil
6   ounces jerk seasoning
3   tablespoons extra-virgin olive oil

For the Fresh Fruit Salsa, combine the pineapple, mango, papaya, jalapeño pepper, lime juice and salt in a bowl and mix well.

For the Tuna, heat a 10- to 12-inch stainless steel skillet over medium-high heat for 2 minutes.

Meanwhile, rub the tuna with 1 tablespoon olive oil. Coat both sides of the tuna with the jerk seasoning.

Pour 3 tablespoons olive oil carefully into the hot skillet and wait for about 30 seconds for the oil to get hot. Add the tuna and cook for about 2 minutes per side, depending on the thickness of the steaks. (Seared tuna is best when served medium-rare.)

To plate, remove each tuna steak to a serving plate. Spoon equal portions of the Fresh Fruit Salsa onto each plate. May serve the tuna over steamed rice or coconut rice.

Note: Jerk seasoning can be found in the ethnic section of the grocery store.

Yield: 2 servings

CHEF ROBERTO HERNANDEZ

Rosemary Beach

*Named one of America's most romantic small towns, Rosemary Beach packs a lot of charm into a small spot.
Unique West Indies–style architecture transports you beyond Florida,
but southern hospitality is still prevalent.*

THE LOWDOWN   Whether you're visiting for the day or a week, you'll want to come back to Rosemary Beach. Go shopping at the boutiques, featuring home goods, makeup and fragrances, books, and even toys. Play a game of bocce or croquet, or stroll down Scenic Highway 30A and visit neighboring Seacrest Beach.

WHAT'S NEARBY   Restaurant Paradis, 82 South Barrett Square (seafood); La Crema, 38 Main Street (tapas, chocolate); Rose Bros., 78 Main Street (burgers, soda fountain).

BEST BEACH . . .   to not see. You may not have access to the beach, but everything else around you will suffice.

BEACH ACCESS   Private, but you can check out the views at the end of the town square.

Grouper Paradis

Grilled Grouper over a Lobster and Fennel Orzo Salad with Roasted Pattypan Squash and a Meyer Lemon Beurre Blanc.

LOBSTER AND FENNEL ORZO SALAD

16 ounces orzo	1 fennel bulb, shaved
1/4 cup olive oil	1 garlic clove, minced
2 1/2 cups warm water	12 ounces precooked lobster
Olive oil	knuckle and claw meat
Butter	Salt and pepper to taste
1 red onion, julienned	

MEYER LEMON BEURRE BLANC

1 shallot, chopped	2 tablespoons heavy cream
1 garlic clove	1 cup (2 sticks) unsalted
1 Meyer lemon	butter, at room
3 sprigs of fresh thyme	temperature, cut into
4 peppercorns	small pieces
2 cups white wine	Salt to taste

ROASTED PATTYPAN SQUASH

12 pattypan squash	Salt and pepper to taste
Olive oil	

GRILLED GROUPER

4 (6-ounce) black grouper	Salt and pepper to taste
fillets	Nonstick cooking spray

CHEF MARK EICHIN

For the Lobster and Fennel Orzo Salad, sauté the orzo in 1/4 cup olive oil in a rondeau pan or deep skillet until light brown. Add the warm water. Bring to a boil; cover. Turn off the heat. Let stand for 10 minutes. Remove to a bowl and let stand to cool.

Heat a small amount of olive oil and a spoonful of butter in a large sauté pan over medium-high heat. Add the onion, fennel and garlic. Sauté until tender. Add the lobster and orzo. Season with salt and pepper.

38

For the Meyer Lemon Beurre Blanc, cook the shallot, garlic, Meyer lemon, thyme and peppercorns in a saucepan until the moisture is released. Add the wine. Cook until reduced to au sec, stirring frequently. Add the heavy cream. Cook until thick and creamy, stirring frequently. Add the butter a piece at a time, whisking constantly. Season with salt. Strain through a fine mesh sieve. Keep warm.

For the Roasted Pattypan Squash, preheat the oven to 400 degrees. Cut off the ends of the squash. Toss the squash in a small amount of olive oil, salt and pepper. Arrange on a baking sheet. Bake for 10 to 15 minutes or until cooked through.

For the Grilled Grouper, season the grouper lightly with salt and pepper and spray with nonstick cooking spray. Grill until cooked through.

To plate, spoon a fourth of the Lobster and Fennel Orzo Salad onto a plate and top with a grouper fillet. Add 3 squash to the plate. Serve with the Meyer Lemon Beurre Blanc.

Yield: 4 servings

RESTAURANT PARADIS

Sandestin

What if you could have room service at the beach? At Hilton Sandestin, you pretty much can.
The private beach access is located in front of the Hilton resort, which is part of Sandestin Golf and Beach Resort.
Anything you need for a day at the beach is provided by beach services. Just bring yourself.

THE LOWDOWN   Sandestin Golf and Beach Resort almost feels like its own private beachfront bubble. Everything you need is nearby: a spa, pool, restaurants, and shopping. And the beach is no exception. It even has its own lifeguard tower. As a guest, you don't even have to get in the car to cross U.S. Highway 98 to visit the shops and attractions at Baytowne Wharf—just take a shuttle.

WHAT'S NEARBY   Seagar's Prime Steaks and Seafood, 4000 South Sandestin Boulevard (surf and turf); Sandcastles Restaurant, 4000 South Sandestin Boulevard (American); Hadashi Sushi Bar, 4000 South Sandestin Boulevard (sushi, Japanese cuisine).

BEST BEACH . . .   to get pampered. See above.

BEACH ACCESS   Private, but you can check out the views from the boardwalk.

Scallops with Creamy Grits, Honey Lime Glaze and Charred Green Onions

CHARRED GREEN ONIONS

2   ounces green onions

CREAMY GRITS

1   cup milk
2   ounces yellow stone ground grits
2   ounces white stone ground grits
Salt and pepper to taste
1   ounce aged white Cheddar cheese, shredded
3   tablespoons butter, chopped, softened

HONEY LIME GLAZE

3   ounces honey
Zest and juice of 1 lime

SCALLOPS

2   tablespoons vegetable oil
4   (10/20) scallops
Salt and pepper to taste
3   tablespoons butter, chopped, softened

For the Charred Green Onions, arrange the green onions on a baking sheet and broil until charred. Let stand to cool. Cut into 1/4-inch slices.

For the Creamy Grits, bring the milk to a boil in a saucepan. Add the yellow grits and white grits. Cook until the mixture reaches the boiling point, stirring constantly. Cover the saucepan. Reduce the heat to low and simmer for 12 to 15 minutes, stirring occasionally and seasoning with salt and pepper during the last 3 minutes of cooking. Remove from the heat. Stir in the Cheddar cheese, Charred Green Onions and butter. Adjust the seasonings.

For the Honey Lime Glaze, combine the honey, lime zest and lime juice in a saucepan. Bring to a simmer. Cook until reduced by half, stirring frequently. Remove from the heat.

For the Scallops, heat a sauté pan over medium-high heat. Add the vegetable oil. Season the scallops with salt and pepper and place carefully in the hot oil. Cook until the edges are golden brown. Turn over the scallops and add the butter. Cook until the butter is melted. Spoon the butter and pan drippings over the scallops. Cook for 2 to 3 minutes or until cooked through.

To plate, spoon half the Creamy Grits and half the Scallops onto a plate. Spoon the Honey Lime Glaze over the scallops. Serve immediately.

Yield: 2 servings

CHEF DAN VARGO

SEAGAR'S PRIME STEAKS AND SEAFOOD

Santa Rosa Beach

Here's the confusing part about Santa Rosa Beach: it technically encompasses several of the beach communities in South Walton. Seagrove, Blue Mountain, and Gulf Place all have Santa Rosa Beach mailing addresses. But it does have its own separate charm. Founded in 1910, Santa Rosa Beach is a little bit of old Florida and new. You also have the choice to venture off of Scenic Highway 30A to explore restaurants and attractions on U.S. Highway 98.

THE LOWDOWN   Because of its size, Santa Rosa Beach has a lot to offer. Beyond the beach, there's Point Washington State Forest and Deer Lake State Park. And there are plenty of beach accesses to choose from.

WHAT'S NEARBY   Local Catch, 3711 West Scenic Highway 30A (seafood); Donut Hole, 6745 U.S. Highway 98 West (American breakfast); Grayton Beer Company, 217 Serenoa Road.

BEST BEACH . . .   to be hidden. There are plenty of neighborhood accesses to walk to and get lost in.

BEACH ACCESS   Gulfview Heights Regional Beach Access, 186 Gulfview Heights Street.

OTHER ACCESS   Van Ness Butler Jr. Regional Beach Access, 1931 East Scenic Highway 30A. Restrooms, parking, beach conditions flag, ADA accessible.

Jumbo Lump Crab Cakes with a Sweet Gastrique and Crystal Beurre Blanc Sauce

CRAB CAKES

1	pound fresh jumbo lump crabmeat
2	eggs
1	cup panko bread crumbs
1/4	cup Creole mustard
1	small red bell pepper, chopped
1	bunch green onions, thinly sliced

Juice of 1 lemon

1	tablespoon Cajun seasoning
2	tablespoons Crystal hot sauce

Vegetable oil for frying

SWEET GASTRIQUE

1	cup white vinegar
1	cup honey

CRYSTAL BEURRE BLANC SAUCE

1	cup Crystal hot sauce
1/4	cup heavy cream
4	tablespoons unsalted butter, cut into small pieces

For the Crab Cakes, preheat the oven to 350 degrees.

Combine the crabmeat, eggs, panko, Creole mustard, red bell pepper, green onions, lemon juice, Cajun seasoning and hot sauce in a bowl and mix well. Shape into 4-ounce patties.

Pour enough vegetable oil into a medium ovenproof sauté pan to lightly cover the bottom. Heat over medium-high heat. Place the crab cakes in the pan and cook for 2 to 3 minutes or until the bottom is seared. Turn over the crab cakes. Bake for 3 minutes or until cooked through.

For the Sweet Gastrique, combine the vinegar and honey in a small saucepan. Cook over medium-low heat until reduced by half, stirring frequently.

For the Crystal Beurre Blanc Sauce, pour the hot sauce into a saucepan. Cook over medium heat until reduced by half.

CHEF ADAM YELLIN

Add the heavy cream and stir to mix. Add the butter. Remove from the heat and stir until the butter is melted.

To plate, spoon Crystal Beurre Blanc Sauce onto a plate in a semicircular pattern. Place a Crab Cake on top. Ladle Sweet Gastrique over the Crab Cake.

Yield: 4 or 5 servings

Seacrest Beach

You don't have to leave Seacrest Beach to have an adventure. The beach, a lake, trails—
it's all part of the Seacrest community. Homes and rental properties are tucked away,
and the private beach access is exclusive to homeowners and guests.

THE LOWDOWN   Established in 1996, the Seacrest Beach community has everything you want or need for your beach vacation with 1.3 miles of unmarked trails, lagoon and beach views, Camp Creek Lake, and a 12,000-square-foot pool. Have you packed your bags yet?

WHAT'S NEARBY   La Cocina, 10343 East Scenic Highway 30A (Mexican); 30A Bagels & Coffee, 10343 East Scenic Highway 30A (breakfast sandwiches, coffee); SeaCrust Pizza, 10343 East Scenic Highway 30A (salads, pizza).

BEST BEACH . . .   to do nothing. The 78-acre community has plenty of places to relax and enjoy quiet time.

BEACH ACCESS   Private.

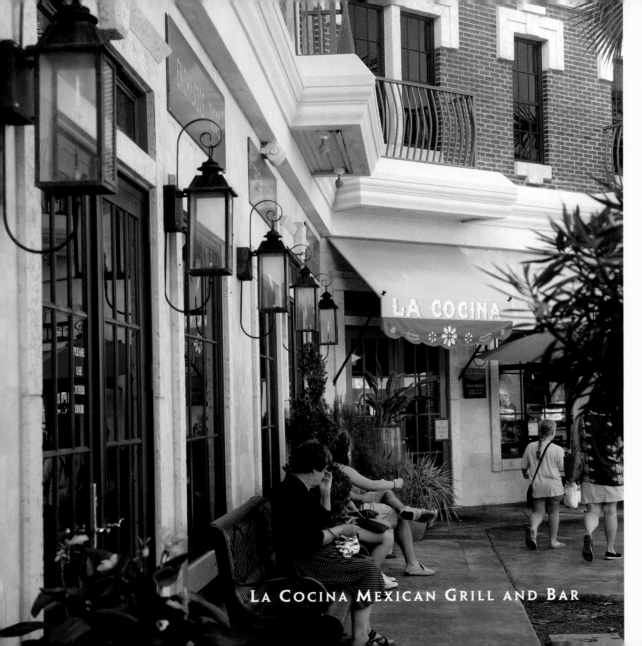

La Cocina Mexican Grill and Bar

La Cocina Fish Tacos

POBLANO LIME TARTAR SAUCE
3   ounces mayonnaise
1 1/4 teaspoons puréed jalapeño pepper
1/8   roasted poblano pepper, chopped
Juice of 1/4 lime
1/8   teaspoon salt
1/8   teaspoon pepper

FISH TACOS
2   (3-ounce) red snapper fillets
Seafood seasoning
2   flour tortillas
Spring lettuce mix
4   slices of tomato
Chopped fresh cilantro

For the Poblano Lime Tartar Sauce, combine the mayonnaise, jalapeño pepper, poblano pepper, lime juice, salt and pepper in a small bowl and mix well. Chill, covered, until serving time.

For the Fish Tacos, season the red snapper fillets with seafood seasoning and grill until the fillets are cooked through. Chargrill the flour tortillas just until warm. Spread each tortilla with half the Poblano Lime Tartar Sauce. Add spring lettuce mix, 2 tomato slices, a fillet and a generous amount of cilantro to each taco. Serve with salsa.

Yield: 1 serving

CHEF ADAM DENNIS

Seagrove Beach

Seagrove Beach offers a little bit of everything:
from two coastal dune lakes to unique shopping and dining experiences, and Deer Lake State Park.

THE LOWDOWN   Seagrove is an in-between spot. It mixes the laid-back Florida lifestyle with the upscale and unique dining and shopping that represent much of Scenic Highway 30A. It's also situated between WaterColor and Seaside, as well as Eastern Lake and Western Lake, offering new experiences to explore.

WHAT'S NEARBY   Old Florida Fish House, 5235 East Scenic Highway 30A (seafood); V Seagrove, 2743 East Scenic Highway 30A (steak, seafood); 723 Whiskey Bravo, 3031 East Scenic Highway 30A (American, seafood).

BEST BEACH . . .   to find your balance. Seagrove Beach is a mix of old and new Florida with plenty of untouched nature to explore at Point Washington State Forest, as well as shops and restaurants to enjoy. Seagrove is a small area with just a mile and a half of beach, but it packs a lot of fun.

BEACH ACCESS   Santa Clara Regional Beach Access, 3468 East Scenic Highway 30A.

OTHER ACCESSES   Dothan Avenue Neighborhood Beach Access, intersection of Dothan Avenue and Montgomery Street; One Seagrove Neighborhood Beach Access, 57 Seagrove Place.

Seascape

Seascape is for the active. Tennis courts, jogging trails, golf courses, and five swimming pools—
not to mention the number one reason for visiting, which is the beach right across the road.

THE LOWDOWN Seascape Golf, Beach & Tennis Resort is a community of condominium rentals located on Scenic Highway 98. You can stay inside the bubble and enjoy all of the resort's amenities or take a free shuttle to a nearby destination. Guests can use free beach service during their stay and walk over to the beach without having to worry about parking.

WHAT'S NEARBY Royal Palm Grille, 1096 Scenic Gulf Drive (fine dining, seafood, steak); The Whale's Tail, 1373 Scenic Gulf Drive (American, seafood); Cabana Cafe, 112 Seascape Boulevard (American).

BEST BEACH . . . safety. With the Walton County Sheriff's Office patrolling the resort, you don't have to worry about Spring Break riffraff.

BEACH ACCESS The beach service is available to guests, but the public entrance is just several feet away next to The Whale's Tail.

Scampi à la Provencal

1   tablespoon olive oil
1   pound shrimp, shelled and deveined
1   shallot, chopped
2   garlic cloves, chopped
1   tomato, peeled, seeded and chopped
2   tablespoons dry white wine

1   tablespoon fresh lemon juice
6   tablespoons butter, cut into 6 pieces, at room temperature
3   tablespoons chopped fresh parsley
1   tablespoon chopped fresh basil
Salt and pepper to taste

Heat the olive oil in a skillet over medium-high heat. Add the shrimp. Cook just until the shrimp turn pink, turning frequently. Add the shallot, garlic and tomato. Cook for 1 to 2 minutes, stirring frequently. Stir in the wine and lemon juice. Reduce the heat. Cook, adding 4 pieces of the butter one at a time and stirring until the butter is incorporated after each addition. Remove from the heat. Add the remaining butter and stir to incorporate. Stir in the parsley, basil, salt and pepper.

To plate, spoon a fourth of the shrimp mixture into a bowl and serve immediately with lots of French bread on the side.

Note: The scampi may be served over pasta or rice.

Yield: 4 servings

EXECUTIVE CHEF MARK HALL AND
SUSHI CHEF ARNEL PAPA

Seaside

Seaside is the most recognized of the sixteen South Walton beaches, most likely because of the 1998 film
The Truman Show, *starring Jim Carrey. While you can purchase the DVD at Central Square Records or*
check out pictures from the set inside Modica Market, the community is more comfortable
being known for its charming architecture and its friendly atmosphere.

THE LOWDOWN   Seaside is a place you can visit even if you don't plan on going to the beach. There's plenty to see as you stroll around the streets, including unique shops and good eats. You might have to circle around before you find a good parking spot, but once you do, you'll have plenty to see. And the beach is as pretty as the rest of the town.

WHAT'S NEARBY   Bud & Alley's, 2236 East Scenic Highway 30A (seafood); Raw and Juicy, located in the front of Central Square (smoothies, snacks); Great Southern Café, 83 Central Square (southern).

BEST BEACH . . .   backstory. Robert and Daryl Davis built a community from the eighty acres that Robert inherited from his grandfather. Inspired by the beach vacations he had as a child, Robert developed Seaside in 1981, a town "seamlessly tied by a common sense of community," according to the website.

BEACH ACCESS   Right in the heart of the town square.

BUD & ALLEY'S
WATERFRONT RESTAURANT

Seaside Shrimp

1	teaspoon chopped fresh rosemary		1/4	cup canola oil
1/2	teaspoon chopped fresh thyme		1/4	cup white wine
1	teaspoon chopped garlic		1	tablespoon lemon juice
1	tablespoon chopped shallot		2	roasted Roma tomatoes, peeled, seeded and coarsely chopped
1/4	teaspoon cracked black pepper		1/2	cup shrimp stock
2	tablespoons canola oil		4	tablespoons cold butter
8	large shrimp, peeled, heads and tails intact			Kosher salt to taste

Combine the rosemary, thyme, garlic, shallot, pepper and 2 tablespoons canola oil in a bowl and mix well. Add the shrimp and stir gently to coat. Marinate in the refrigerator for 1 hour. Heat a medium skillet over medium-high heat. Add 1/4 cup canola oil and sauté the shrimp mixture for about 1 minute or until the shrimp start to turn pink. Deglaze the pan with the white wine. Add the lemon juice, tomatoes and shrimp stock. Cook for 3 to 4 minutes or until the liquid is reduced by half and the shrimp are cooked through, stirring occasionally.

To plate, remove the shrimp to a bowl. Add the butter to the skillet. Cook until the sauce has thickened slightly, stirring constantly. Season with kosher salt. Pour the sauce over the shrimp. Serve with a slice of grilled bread.

Yield: 1 serving

CHEF DAVID BISHOP

WaterColor

It would be hard to check out of WaterColor. Whether you're staying at the resort or enjoying a private rental, the community has just about everything your getaway needs, from luxury services to shopping and dining. The beach is tucked away, but once you get there, it's a breathtaking sight.

THE LOWDOWN
Like most resorts, you don't have to go far (or sometimes anywhere) to enjoy a relaxing day at WaterColor. Amenities such as bike or kayak rentals, spas, and shopping are right there. You can also take a trip on Western Lake or explore Point Washington State Forest.

WHAT'S NEARBY
Fish Out of Water, 34 Goldenrod Circle (American, Creole, seafood, and more); The Candy Bar, 1777 East Scenic Highway 30A (ice cream, candy); Wine World, 1735 East Scenic Highway 30A (tapas, wine).

BEST BEACH . . .
to not be on the beach. WaterColor's pool gives you the view of the Gulf without having to step in the sand.

BEACH ACCESS
Private.

WaterSound

When you truly want to get away, choose the beach at WaterSound as your getaway.
The enclosed community sets you apart from the world and lets the relaxation settle in.

THE LOWDOWN   The gated beachfront community mixes luxury resort styles with back-to-basics nature. Trails, pedestrian bridges, and boardwalks lead you to the private beach. You can also take advantage of four uniquely designed pools, parks, a putt-putt course, and even a shallow pond for remote-controlled boats.

WHAT'S NEARBY   Bruno's Pizza, 6652 East Scenic Highway 30A (pizza, grinders); WaterSound Origins Cafe, 530 Pathways Drive (American); The Hub, 6910 East Scenic Highway 30A (burgers, ice cream, tacos).

BEST BEACH . . .   to not be found. If you want seclusion, it comes free at WaterSound.

BEACH ACCESS   Private.

BRUNO'S PIZZA

Garlic Knots

2   *(10-count) cans refrigerator biscuits*
1   *cup (2 sticks) butter, melted*
4   *ounces minced garlic*
4   *ounces grated Parmesan cheese*
4   *ounces marinara sauce*

Preheat the oven to 400 degrees.

Cut the biscuits into halves and shape each half into a ball. Arrange 2 inches apart on an ungreased baking sheet. Bake for 12 to 15 minutes or until golden brown.

Place the knots in a large bowl. Add the butter and garlic. Toss the knots lightly to coat. Sprinkle with the Parmesan cheese. Arrange on a serving platter and serve with the marinara sauce.

Yield: 40 knots

CHEF JEFF GOODMAN

Beaches of Destin

Crystal Beach

Away from U.S. Highway 98 and right where you want to be—on the Gulf.
The Shores at Crystal Beach Park is a nook for beach lovers.

THE LOWDOWN   Located among the homes and rental units on Crystal Beach, the park is a perfect walk-up spot to enjoy the beach. A few parking spots are available for guests who are driving by.

WHAT'S NEARBY   Camille's at Crystal Beach, 2931 Scenic Highway 98 (sushi, seafood); 790 on the Gulf, 2996 Scenic Highway 98 (Cajun cuisine, fresh Gulf seafood); O'Quigley's Seafood Steamer & Oyster Sports Bar, 34940 Emerald Coast Parkway, #101 (seafood, steaks, all-American pub food).

BEST BEACH . . .   for a walk. Stroll around the fancy, pastel homes in Crystal Beach when you're done at the beach.

BEACH ACCESS   The Shores at Crystal Beach Park, 2966 Scenic Highway 98.

OTHER ACCESSES   Barracuda and Scenic Highway 98; Crystal Beach Drive and Scenic Highway 98; Shirah Street and Scenic Highway 98; 7th Street and Scenic Highway 98; Tarpon Street and Scenic Highway 98; Pompano Street and Scenic Highway 98. These locations feature walkovers only.

CAMILLE'S AT CRYSTAL BEACH

Baked Avocado

2   tablespoons mayonnaise
1/2   teaspoon sambal chili paste
1   avocado, cut into halves
Fresh lemon juice
Soy sauce

Preheat the oven to 350 degrees.

Combine the mayonnaise and chili paste in a small bowl and mix well to make a sauce.

Place the avocado halves in a baking dish. Sprinkle with lemon juice. Drizzle with soy sauce. Top with the sauce.

Bake for 4 to 5 minutes or until golden brown. Arrange on a serving plate.

Yield: 1 serving

CHEF MISCHA PAWLIK

East Pass

Veer to the right before you jump onto Marler Bridge entering Destin.
You'll find East Pass, a small beach spot that features a good view and solitude.

THE LOWDOWN
East Pass is more known to locals as a spot to relax by yourself, watch the traffic at Crab Island, or have a quiet walk along the water. It's a throwback to the time when beaches were little else but sand, water, and fun.

WHAT'S NEARBY
Jackacudas Seafood & Sushi, 56 Harbor Boulevard (local Gulf to table dining, sushi); Harry T's, 46 Harbor Boulevard (American); AJ's Seafood & Oyster Bar, 116 Harbor Boulevard (seafood, fresh oysters, surf and turf).

BEST BEACH . . .
to hide on. Work on a tan, read a book—you won't be bothered.

BEACH ACCESS
West end of Santa Rosa Island, East U.S. Highway 98 and Destin's Marler Bridge.

Lump Crab and Parmesan-Crusted Gulf Snapper

CREAMED PESTO

2   garlic cloves
1/3   cup pine nuts
4   cups fresh basil leaves

1/2   cup extra-virgin olive oil
1/2   cup grated Parmesan cheese
1 1/2 cups heavy cream

SUNBURST HEIRLOOM TOMATO AND ASPARAGUS RISOTTO

6   cups chicken broth
1   tablespoon extra-virgin olive oil
1   pint baby heirloom tomatoes
5   large asparagus, cut into thin slices
     diagonally
1   tablespoon extra-virgin olive oil

1   shallot, diced
1 1/2 cups arborio rice
1/2   cup white wine
3   tablespoons butter, softened
1/3   cup grated Parmesan cheese
1/4   cup coarsely chopped parsley

GULF SNAPPER

2   cups panko bread crumbs
1   cup grated Parmesan cheese
1/4   cup butter, melted
1/4   cup coarsely chopped parsley
1 1/2 tablespoons granulated garlic
1/2   tablespoon granulated onion

8   ounces lump crabmeat
4   (8-ounce) Gulf snapper fillets
Nonstick cooking spray
1   tablespoon butter, softened
3/4   cup water

CHEF ALLEN TEUTON

For the Creamed Pesto, combine the garlic, pine nuts and basil in a food processor and pulse until the ingredients stick to the wall of the food processor bowl. Add the olive oil and Parmesan cheese and pulse until mixed. Season with salt and pepper. This can be made a day ahead of time and stored in the refrigerator. Heat the cream in a medium sauté pan until reduced by a third. Add 2 tablespoons of the pesto to the cream and mix well.

For the Sunburst Heirloom Tomato and Asparagus Risotto, bring the chicken broth just to the boiling point in a medium saucepan. Heat 1 tablespoon olive oil in a large saucepan. Sauté the tomatoes and asparagus in the olive oil until the asparagus is cooked through and the tomatoes start to break down. Pour into a small bowl and reserve. Add 1 tablespoon olive oil to the saucepan. Sauté the shallot in the olive oil until translucent. Add the rice and stir with a wooden spoon until all of the rice is coated with the olive oil. Cook for 2 minutes, stirring constantly. Add the wine and cook until all of the wine is absorbed, stirring constantly. Cook for 17 to 20 minutes, adding the chicken broth 1/2 cup at a time and stirring until the broth is absorbed after each addition. Cook until the rice is al dente, adding additional broth if additional cooking time is needed. Remove from the heat. Stir in the butter, Parmesan cheese and parsley. Add the reserved tomato mixture and mix gently. Season with salt and pepper.

For the Gulf Snapper, preheat the oven to 375 degrees. Turn the fan on low if using a convection oven. Combine the panko, Parmesan cheese, melted butter, parsley, garlic and onion in a small bowl and stir until the mixture retains its shape, adding additional melted butter if needed. Add the crabmeat carefully, taking care not to break the lumps apart. Season the snapper fillets with salt and pepper. Spoon equal portions of the panko mixture onto each fillet, pressing firmly. Spray a small baking pan with cooking spray. Arrange the fillets at least 1 inch apart in the baking pan. Add the softened butter and water to the pan. Bake for 9 to 12 minutes or until golden brown and a wooden pick inserted into the center of the fillets goes through easily.

To plate, scoop a few large spoonfuls of the Sunburst Heirloom Tomato and Asparagus Risotto onto a large plate, making sure to get an even amount of tomatoes. Tap the bottom of the plate to distribute the risotto evenly. Spoon 3 tablespoonfuls of the Creamed Pesto around the risotto. Remove a Gulf Snapper fillet from the baking pan using a fish spatula and place on the center of the risotto. Enjoy!

Yield: 4 servings

JACKACUDAS SEAFOOD & SUSHI

Henderson Beach State Park

Appreciate nature in its purest form at Henderson Beach State Park,
which features 6,000 feet of untouched shoreline.
You won't believe you're just minutes away from the upscale homes and neighborhoods of Destin.

THE LOWDOWN   There's a price to pay at Henderson Beach State Park ($2-$6), but it's well worth it. You're in a quiet getaway, complete with trails, camping, and a playground. Enjoy the beach with the condominiums in the distance.

WHAT'S NEARBY   Beach Walk Cafe, 2700 Scenic Highway 98 (American); Fudpucker's, 20001 Emerald Coast Parkway (American, seafood); Destin Commons, 4100 Legendary Drive.

BEST BEACH . . .   to explore. There are tall dunes, walking trails, and plenty of wildlife to view. Ask a park ranger how to make the most of your stay.

BEACH ACCESS   17000 Emerald Coast Parkway.

Magnolia Grill
magnoliagrillfwb.com

Chipotle Barbecue Shrimp and Grits

CHIPOTLE BARBECUE CREAM SAUCE

1/2	white onion, chopped
1	ounce minced garlic
1	tablespoon vegetable oil
2	ounces chipotle peppers
1 1/4 cups ketchup	
1	ounce Dijon mustard
1	cup Worcestershire sauce
1/2	cup red wine vinegar

1/2	cup lemon juice
3/4	cup packed brown sugar
1	cup water
2	teaspoons chicken base
2	teaspoons kosher salt
2	teaspoons coarsely ground black pepper
2	cups heavy cream

SMOKED GOUDA CHEESE GRITS

2	cups heavy cream
2	cups water
1/2	tablespoon chicken base

1	cup grits
4	ounces smoked Gouda cheese, chopped
1/2	teaspoon kosher salt
1/2	teaspoon black pepper

SHRIMP

2	tablespoons vegetable oil
1	red bell pepper, julienned
1	green bell pepper, julienned
1	red onion, julienned

1	garlic clove, minced
4	ounces andouille sausage, chopped
1	pound (31/35) shrimp

CHEF JOE MARLOW

For the Chipotle Barbecue Cream Sauce, sauté the onion and garlic in the vegetable oil in a large saucepan over medium-high heat until the onion is translucent. Add the chipotle peppers and sauté for 1 minute. Add the ketchup, Dijon mustard, Worcestershire sauce, vinegar, lemon juice, brown sugar, water, chicken base, salt and pepper and mix well. Bring to a boil. Reduce the heat to low and simmer for 30 minutes, stirring occasionally. Add the heavy cream and bring to a boil. Reduce the heat to low and simmer for 15 minutes, stirring occasionally. Remove from the heat. Purée using an immersion blender until smooth.

For the Smoked Gouda Cheese Grits, combine the heavy cream, water and chicken base in a large saucepan and bring to a boil. Whisk in the grits and mix well. Bring to a boil. Stir the Gouda cheese into the grits. Add the salt and pepper and mix well; cover. Let stand for 10 minutes.

For the Shrimp, heat a large sauté pan briefly over medium-high heat. Add the vegetable oil. Sauté the red bell pepper, green bell pepper, onion, garlic and sausage in the oil for 2 to 3 minutes. Add the shrimp and cook for 2 to 3 minutes, stirring occasionally. Add the Chipotle Barbecue Cream Sauce and bring to a boil. Remove from the heat.

To plate, spoon a fourth of the Smoked Gouda Cheese Grits onto the center of a plate. Top with a fourth of the shrimp mixture. Garnish with diagonally sliced scallions.

Yield: 4 servings

BEACH WALK CAFE AT HENDERSON PARK INN

81

James Lee Park

You have your pick of spots, and you're just a short walk away from lunch at James Lee Park.

THE LOWDOWN   The last beach before you hit Walton County, James Lee Park is a good size for any beach group and has plenty of parking, a walkover, outdoor showers, restrooms, and a lifeguard tower. If you're hungry, you can pack a lunch and enjoy it at the picnic area or walk over to The Crab Trap.

WHAT'S NEARBY   The Crab Trap, 3500 Scenic Highway 98 (seafood); 790 on the Gulf, 2996 Scenic Highway 98 (seafood); Capt. Dave's on the Gulf, 3796 Scenic Highway 98 (seafood).

BEST BEACH . . .   to be in two places at once. Being close to Walton County, you can check out Miramar Beach.

BEACH ACCESS   3510 Scenic Highway 98.

Crab Trap Crab Cake Dinner

CORN MAQUE CHOUX

4	tablespoons butter
2	cups chopped yellow onions
1/2	cup chopped green onions
1	tablespoon minced garlic
1	red bell pepper, chopped
1/4	cup chopped fresh parsley
1	teaspoon black pepper

1/2	teaspoon cayenne pepper
1/2	teaspoon Florida Bay Seasoning
1/2	ounce crab base
3	cups corn
2	cups chopped andouille sausage
1 3/4	cups heavy cream
Salt to taste	

CRAB CAKES

1/4	cup chopped celery
1/4	cup chopped green bell pepper
1/3	cup chopped green onions
4	egg yolks
2	tablespoons heavy cream
1	tablespoon Florida Bay Seasoning
1 1/2	teaspoons granulated garlic (not garlic salt)
1 1/2	teaspoons baking powder

1 1/2	teaspoons Worcestershire sauce
1	ounce crab base
1	pound jumbo lump crabmeat
1	pound crab claw meat
1	cup panko bread crumbs
Vegetable oil for frying	
Buttermilk	
Seafood breading	

FRIED GREEN TOMATOES

Green tomatoes, sliced
All-purpose flour

Buttermilk
White cornmeal

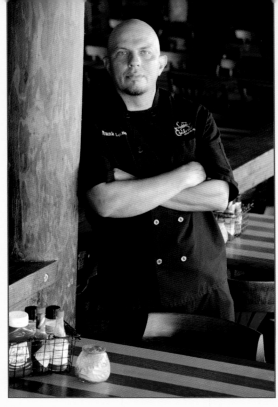

CHEF FRANK LOZANO

For the Corn Maque Choux, melt the butter in a large saucepan over medium-high heat. Add the yellow onions, green onions, garlic, red bell pepper, parsley, black pepper, cayenne pepper, Florida Bay Seasoning, crab base, corn and sausage. Cook until the vegetables are tender, stirring occasionally. Add the heavy cream and salt and mix well.

For the Crab Cakes, combine the celery, bell pepper, green onions, egg yolks, heavy cream, Florida Bay Seasoning, garlic, baking powder, Worcestershire sauce and crab base in a large bowl and mix well. Add the lump crabmeat and the crab claw meat and mix gently. Add the panko and mix gently.

Heat the vegetable oil to 350 degrees in a deep fryer or electric skillet. Shape the crab mixture into 3-ounce patties. Dip the patties into buttermilk and coat with seafood breading. Fry until golden brown. Remove to paper towels to drain.

For the Fried Green Tomatoes, coat the green tomatoes with flour and dip in buttermilk. Coat with cornmeal. Fry in the deep fryer until golden brown.

To plate, spoon about 1/2 cup of Corn Maque Choux onto a plate. Place 2 Fried Green Tomatoes on top of the Corn Maque Choux. Arrange 2 Crab Cakes on top of the Fried Green Tomatoes. Garnish with rémoulade sauce and green onions.

Yield: 6 or 7 servings

THE CRAB TRAP SEAFOOD AND OYSTER BAR

June White Decker Park

When you want to go to lunch and head to the beach (or vice versa),
June White Decker Park is a good spot to dine and dash—to the beach.

THE LOWDOWN

At the end of Restaurant Road on Scenic Highway 98, June White Decker Park has parking and all the regular beach amenities you'd want, including showers, restrooms, and a walkover. You're not a long walk away from the beach, unlike some of the more popular spots.

WHAT'S NEARBY

The Back Porch, 1740 Scenic Highway 98 (seafood, American); Candymaker, 1771 Scenic Highway 98 (breakfast, sweets); Destin Diner, 1083 U.S. Highway 98 (American).

BEST BEACH . . .

for lunch or brunch. Restaurants are just a short walk away.

BEACH ACCESS

Scenic Highway 98, south end of Restaurant Road.

OTHER ACCESSES

Calhoun Beach Access, Scenic Highway 98 (Restaurant Road); Silver Shells, 7th Street and Scenic Highway 98.

THE BACK PORCH SEAFOOD
& OYSTER HOUSE

Back Porch Key Lime Pie

1	(14-ounce) can sweetened condensed milk
4	large egg yolks
5	ounces key lime juice
1	(9-inch) graham cracker pie shell

Preheat the oven to 250 degrees. Combine the sweetened condensed milk and egg yolks in a metal bowl and whisk to mix. Add the key lime juice, whisking until well mixed. Spoon into the pie shell.

Bake for 10 minutes (do not brown). Let stand at room temperature for 2 minutes. Chill in the refrigerator for 3 hours or until very cold. Garnish with whipped cream and lime slices.

Yield: 6 to 8 servings

CHEF IAN BARBER

Norriego Point

Tucked away from U.S. Highway 98, Norriego Point is a trip to "old Destin."
You notice it in the vintage signage you see when you're driving through Holiday Isle.

THE LOWDOWN   There are no restrooms or showers and not much parking, but Norriego Point offers a perfect view of boats going back and forth from the Destin harbor. You'll also see the pirate cruise ship coming through. Stroll down the walking path and take in the quaint neighborhoods.

WHAT'S NEARBY   Louisiana Lagniappe, 775 Gulf Shore Drive (Creole); La Paz, 950 Gulf Shore Drive (Mexican); Bric à Brac, 824 U.S. Highway 98 (Cajun, seafood).

BEST BEACH . . .   to travel back in time. With views of Emerald Grande, you won't forget what year it is, but the old condominiums and the quiet road will make you think about yesteryear.

BEACH ACCESS   Gulf Shore Drive.

OTHER ACCESS   O'Steen Public Beach Access, Gulf Shore Drive.

Louisiana Lagniappe Restaurant

Bread Pudding

1	(8-count) package hamburger buns	2	cups sugar
2	(14-ounce) cans fruit cocktail, drained	1	cup (2 sticks) salted butter
6	eggs	1	tablespoon ground cinnamon
2	cups evaporated milk	1 1/2	cups pecan pieces
5	cups whole milk		

CHEF MIKE DIEUADE

Preheat the oven to 325 degrees.

Tear the hamburger buns into small pieces. Combine the bread and fruit cocktail in a 9×13-inch baking pan and spread evenly.

Combine the eggs and evaporated milk in a large bowl and whisk to mix well. Add the whole milk and whisk to mix well. Add the sugar and whisk until the sugar is dissolved.

Melt the butter in a bowl in the microwave. Add to the milk mixture and whisk briskly. Pour over the bread mixture and whisk for 2 minutes. Sprinkle with the cinnamon and mix gently. Spread evenly and sprinkle the pecans over the top.

Bake for 30 to 35 minutes. Rotate the baking pan a half turn. Bake for 5 to 10 minutes or until the center is puffy (do not overbrown). Let stand at room temperature until the center of the pudding falls. Place on a wire rack to cool completely. Cut into squares and enjoy!

Yield: 6 to 9 servings

Beaches of Okaloosa Island

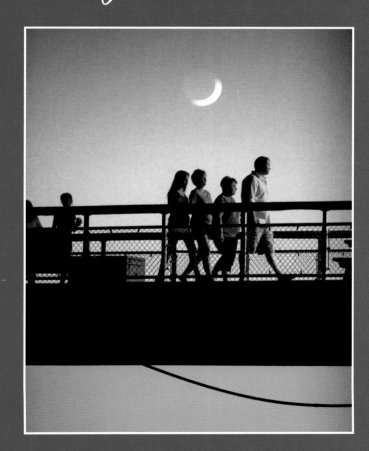

Beasley Park

*When you want to go to the beach, but you don't want to fight for a parking spot
and trudge through the crowds, just head to John Beasley Park.*

THE LOWDOWN   Beasley Park has just about everything you need for your beach stay, including restrooms and shaded pavilions. It's not so secluded that you don't have a lifeguard or views of The Boardwalk, but it's set off enough to enjoy some peace and quiet.

WHAT'S NEARBY   Fudpucker's Beachside Bar and Grill, 1318 Miracle Strip Parkway (American, seafood); Asiago's Skillet, 110 Amberjack Drive (Southern breakfast); Yogo Mogos, 1306 Miracle Strip Parkway (frozen yogurt).

BEST BEACH . . .   to separate from the condominiums. The Beasley Park sign is one of the last landmarks heading east on U.S. Highway 98 before you get to Destin.

BEACH ACCESS   1550 Miracle Strip Parkway.

Shrimp Parmesan à la Fud

PARMESAN TOPPING

2   cups mayonnaise

1   cup grated Parmesan cheese

1   teaspoon Father Fud's Secret Seasoning or Tony Chachere's Seasoning

1   tablespoon fresh lemon juice

CRABMEAT STUFFING

1   pound crabmeat (half lump and half claw preferred)

2   green onions, chopped

1   cup cracker meal or finely crushed Ritz crackers

1   tablespoon self-rising flour

1/4   cup mayonnaise

1   egg, beaten

1   teaspoon Father Fud's Secret Seasoning or Tony Chachere's Seasoning

For the Parmesan Topping, combine the mayonnaise, Parmesan cheese, Secret Seasoning and lemon juice in a medium bowl and mix well.

SHRIMP

2   tablespoons butter

24   large shrimp, peeled and deveined, tail intact

2   lemons

1   cup chopped tomatoes

Paprika

1   tablespoon finely chopped fresh parsley or basil

Grated Parmesan cheese

CHEF CHESTER KROEGER

For the Crabmeat Stuffing, combine the crabmeat, green onions, cracker meal, flour, mayonnaise, egg and Secret Seasoning in a medium bowl and mix well. Shape into 1-ounce balls.

For the Shrimp, preheat the oven to 350 degrees. Butter the bottom and sides of four 6- to 7-inch round baking dishes.

Arrange 6 shrimp in a circular pattern in each baking dish. Top each shrimp with a scoop of the Crabmeat Stuffing and fold over the tails. Spoon 1 tablespoon of the Parmesan Topping onto each shrimp.

Cut off the ends of the lemons and cut each lemon into halves. Place a lemon half on its base in the center of each dish and top with 1 tablespoon of the tomatoes. Bake for 12 to 15 minutes or until the shrimp tails begin to darken (do not overcook).

To finish, sprinkle paprika over the shrimp and sprinkle parsley over the tomatoes. Sprinkle Parmesan cheese over the entire dish.

Note: If you have any leftover Crabmeat Stuffing, you may use it to make miniature crab cakes.

Yield: 4 servings

Gulf Islands National Seashore: Okaloosa County

Across the road from the beach is a quiet waterfront view at Gulf Islands National Seashore.
The untouched seashore is a good spot for swimming in calm waters and watching wildlife.

THE LOWDOWN   It's Choctawhatchee Bay, not the beach, but it's still a beautiful view. It's hard to believe that U.S. Highway 98 traffic is zooming behind you as you sit in the sand or go out on the boat. If you go parasailing, you'll see it.

WHAT'S NEARBY   AJ's Oyster Shanty, 108 Santa Rosa Boulevard (seafood, American); Helen Back Cafe, 114 Amberjack Drive (American sports bar, offering pizza and sandwiches); Salvati's Pizza Factory, 1306 Miracle Strip Parkway (pizza, paninis).

BEST BEACH . . .   that's not really the beach. You're at Choctawhatchee Bay, but who cares when you're in paradise?

BEACH ACCESS   Miracle Strip Parkway, Okaloosa Island.

Matterhorn

It's back to basics at what is known as the Matterhorn Beach Access.
This Eglin Air Force Base property is open to the public.
The beach is not much more than sand and white dunes, but you don't need much more.

THE LOWDOWN   Matterhorn is one of three local beaches owned by Eglin Air Force Base. The pristine beach lacks a paved parking lot, which can be tricky to get into with the U.S. Highway 98 traffic, but it's worth it.

WHAT'S NEARBY   Go east and visit HarborWalk Village or head west and grab lunch at The Boardwalk restaurants.

BEST BEACH ...   to fish. Not a lot of competition because it takes a little bit of work to get there.

BEACH ACCESS   Off Miracle Strip Parkway on Santa Rosa Island.

Princess Beach

*Cute name and a beautiful spot. Princess Beach is one of three spots on Santa Rosa Island
owned by Eglin Air Force Base and is open to the public.
It's a bit of a walk in the sand to find your spot, but it's worth it.*

THE LOWDOWN   There's sand and water and not much else, but that's what makes Princess Beach special. Enjoy the open space all by yourself (practically) and pretend you're visiting a lost island.

WHAT'S NEARBY   Backtrack to Okaloosa Island for local favorites, including Pandora's Steakhouse or Old Bay Steamer.

BEST BEACH . . .   to escape. You might be sitting by the busy traffic on U.S. Highway 98, but you won't feel like it.

BEACH ACCESS   Off Miracle Strip Parkway on Santa Rosa Island.

Santa Rosa Boulevard

Drive down Santa Rosa Boulevard on Okaloosa Island, and you'll have your pick
of several small beach accesses, complete with showers, restrooms, pavilions, and parking.
You'll have the opportunity to make new friends when you're sharing the beach with guests at the condominiums.

THE LOWDOWN — A lot of people may flock to The Boardwalk or Beasley Park, but the beach accesses off Santa Rosa Boulevard require less walking from your car to the beach and are slightly more secluded. You also have the option of taking a stroll down the walking path to check out the other accesses.

WHAT'S NEARBY — Old Bay Steamer, 102 Santa Rosa Boulevard (seafood); Pandora's Steak House, 1226 Santa Rosa Boulevard (steak, seafood); Joe & Eddie's Family Restaurant, 1225 Santa Rosa Boulevard (breakfast, American).

BEST BEACH . . . — to beach hop. All of the beach accesses have the same view, but they are close by just in case you want to compare.

BEACH ACCESSES — #1, Blue Dolphin Beachwalk, 372 Santa Rosa Boulevard; #2, Emerald View Beachwalk, 399 Santa Rosa Boulevard; #3, Seashore Beachwalk, 530 Santa Rosa Boulevard; #7, Emerald Promenade Beachwalk, 900 Santa Rosa Boulevard.

OTHER ACCESSES — #4, 600 Santa Rosa Boulevard, Fort Walton Beach; #5, 700 Santa Rosa Boulevard, Fort Walton Beach; #6, Doris Jordan Freeway Beachwalk, 820 Santa Rosa Boulevard, Fort Walton Beach. These locations are neighborhood accesses and walkovers only.

OLD BAY STEAMER
Seafood & Spirits

Seafood Medley

10   ounces angel hair pasta
2   tablespoons butter
3   Gulf shrimp
3   fresh Atlantic sea scallops
3   blue mussels
3   littleneck clams
1/4 cup dry white wine
2   tablespoons seafood base
6   tablespoons tomato sauce
1/4 cup Parmesan cheese
Chopped fresh parsley

Cook the pasta according to the package directions; drain.

Melt the butter in a sauté pan over medium heat. Add the shrimp, scallops, mussels and clams. Sauté until cooked through. Add the wine. Cook until reduced by about half, stirring frequently. Add the seafood base and tomato sauce. Cook for 2 minutes, stirring frequently. Stir in the pasta.

To serve, spoon the pasta into a pasta bowl. Sprinkle with the Parmesan cheese and parsley. Serve with toasted crostini on the side.

Yield: 1 serving

CHEF JEREMY LEIVA

The Boardwalk

Known to longtime locals as Wayside Park, The Boardwalk is the hub of Okaloosa Island with dining, playgrounds, shopping, and, of course, the beach.

THE LOWDOWN   During peak season, The Boardwalk is buzzing with activity (and usually a packed parking lot). It's a popular spot for both visitors and tourists, who want to enjoy a lively day at the beach. And because of the retail shops and restaurants nearby, you really can spend an entire day there.

WHAT'S NEARBY   The Black Pearl, 1450 Miracle Strip Parkway (steak, seafood); The Crab Trap, 1450 Miracle Strip Parkway (seafood); Rockin Tacos, 1450 Miracle Strip Parkway (Mexican).

BEST BEACH . . .   to go home tired. The kids will sleep through the night after a day at The Boardwalk.

BEACH ACCESS   1450 Miracle Strip Parkway.

Designs & Accessories

THE BLACK PEARL
WOOD FIRED SEAFOOD

Blackened Grouper Cheeks

BLACK-EYED PEAS

1	cup dried black-eyed peas
5	to 6 ounces bacon, chopped
1	small white onion, chopped
1¹/3	cups chicken stock

GROUPER CHEEKS

18	grouper cheeks
	Blackening seasoning to taste
1	cup clarified butter (see Note)

For the Black-Eyed Peas, sort and rinse the peas. Combine the peas with enough water to cover in a large bowl and soak overnight; drain.

Cook the bacon and onion in a large pot over medium heat until the bacon releases its fat and the onion is translucent, stirring frequently. Add the peas and chicken stock. Bring to a boil. Reduce the heat and simmer, covered, for 30 to 40 minutes, adding additional chicken stock if needed to keep the peas covered.

For the Grouper Cheeks, coat the grouper cheeks with the blackening seasoning. Heat the clarified butter in a cast-iron skillet over medium-high heat just until smoky. Cook the grouper cheeks in the butter for 3 to 4 minutes or until the bottom is crusty. Turn over the grouper cheeks. Cook for 1 minute.

Serve the Blackened Grouper Cheeks over the Black-eyed Peas and sprinkle with a few chives. May serve with a small mixed green salad.

Note: To make clarified butter, melt 2 cups unsalted butter in a heavy saucepan over low heat. Remove from the heat and let stand for 5 minutes. Skim the foam from the top and slowly pour the clarified butter into a container, discarding the milky solids in the bottom of the pan.

Yield: 6 servings

CHEF KEVIN WYNN

Beaches of Navarre

Gulf Islands National Seashore: Santa Rosa County

Untouched, pristine, and open to the public. You don't always get all three when looking for a beach spot. But Gulf Islands National Seashore provides a quiet spot to relax in nature and soak up the sun.

THE LOWDOWN   The Gulf Islands National Seashore is 160 miles of beach from Cat Island in Mississippi to Okaloosa County in Florida. The seashore is a haven for wildlife because it is protected by park rangers and is kept untouched. While other beaches may have crews do restoration efforts, nature dictates this seashore.

WHAT'S NEARBY   Pensacola Beach and Navarre Beach are just a few miles away, heading west and east respectively.

BEST BEACH . . .   drive. It's a slow-moving twenty-five miles per hour, but the drive along the Gulf Islands National Seashore is a pretty one.

BEACH ACCESSES   In Santa Rosa County, just past the Navarre Beach Marine Park heading west. In Okaloosa County, the park is located just east of Fort Walton Beach on Okaloosa Island.

Navarre Beach

For years, Navarre Beach has gone by the title of "Florida's Best Kept Secret."
But over time, the secret got out. Now, visitors come from all over to enjoy Navarre Beach and all it has to offer.
However, the throwback coastal community has maintained its small-town charm.

THE LOWDOWN Whether you want to hang out at the beach and play volleyball with friends or head to a quiet spot to read your favorite book, there's a spot for everybody on Navarre Beach. And if you don't want to go to the beach at all, you're right by the Santa Rosa Sound, where you can paddleboard or take a jet ski out for a spin. Walk or fish along the Navarre Beach pier, the longest pier in Florida (1,545 feet long and thirty feet above the water), and check out the Gulf Islands National Seashore nearby.

WHAT'S NEARBY Juana's Pagodas and Sailors' Grill, 1451 Navarre Beach Causeway (seafood, American); Lagerheads on the Gulf, 8579 Gulf Boulevard (seafood, American); Helen Back Again, 8651 Navarre Parkway (pizza).

BEST BEACH . . . crowds. The best crowd is no crowd. The old motto for Navarre Beach has been "Florida's Best Kept Secret." And even though tourism has grown, you'll always find a good spot to relax.

BEACH ACCESS Navarre Beach Marine Park, 8740 Gulf Boulevard.

OTHER ACCESS Along Gulf Boulevard. The only amenity is parking.

Juana's Pagodas and Sailors' Grill

Greek Burger

FETA SPREAD

4 ounces feta cheese, crumbled
1/2 teaspoon minced garlic
1/4 teaspoon ground oregano

8 ounces cream cheese
1/4 teaspoon crushed red pepper
Olive pomace oil

CRISPY RED ONION RINGS

1 red onion
House-Autry Onion Ring Coating

Vegetable oil for deep-frying

BURGER

8 ounces certified Angus ground beef
Greek seasoning

1 hamburger bun, toasted
Sliced black olives

CHEF JENNIFER BRYANT

For the Feta Spread, combine the feta cheese, garlic, oregano, cream cheese and red pepper in a mixing bowl. Add the olive oil gradually, beating constantly on low until creamy. Store, covered, in the refrigerator until serving time.

For the Crispy Red Onion Rings, cut the onion into very thin slices and separate into rings. Place the onion rings in a bowl of ice water and let stand for 10 minutes; drain. Coat the onion rings with the Onion Ring Coating. Heat vegetable oil in a deep fryer or saucepan over medium-high heat. Fry the onion rings in the hot oil for 60 seconds or until golden brown.

For the Burger, combine the ground beef and Greek seasoning in a bowl and mix well. Shape into a patty. Cook the burger on a grill to the preferred temperature.

To plate, place the bottom half of the bun on a plate and add the burger. Spread with a scoop of the Feta Spread. Add black olives, Crispy Red Onion Rings and the top of the bun. Enjoy!

Yield: 1 serving

Coastal History

When the Euchee Indians sailed along the Gulf of Mexico coast, it is said that "the great spirit told them to stop."
According to one of our country's origin stories, they ended up calling the place Okaloosa,
a word with several interpretations. To the Euchees, it meant "a pleasant place" or "beautiful place."
They were right, of course…Okaloosa was indeed one of the most beautiful places on earth.

—"Okaloosa County Memories"

At the dawn of the twentieth century, the swamps and forests that would become Okaloosa County were home to isolated pockets of hardworking homesteaders.

In 1915, the year Okaloosa County was born, it wasn't the coastline, but rather north county communities, such as Crestview, Laurel Hill, and Baker, that were considered the most desirable places to live.

Obviously, the times have changed.

The Emerald Coast, the sixty-plus miles of shoreline from Navarre Beach in Santa Rosa County to the famed Beaches of South Walton County, has evolved over the past century and is now dotted with millions of visitors each year, generating a multi-billion dollar industry.

It has been an amazing journey.

Fun Facts

- Okaloosa County was created by an act passed by the Florida House of Representatives on June 3, 1915. Okaloosa is a Choctaw word meaning "black water." "Oka" means water, and "lusa" is black in the Choctaw language.

- Walton County was created in 1824 and named for Colonel George Walton, secretary of West Florida during the territorial governorship of Andrew Jackson. Walton was the son of George Walton, Governor of Georgia and signer of the Declaration of Independence.

- Santa Rosa County was created in 1842, following a land split with Escambia County to the west. According to the Florida Historical Society, it was named for the Roman Catholic saint Rosa de Viterbo.

Destin

Known as the "World's Luckiest Fishing Village," Destin is one of the country's top destinations for tourists.

According to history annals from the City of Destin, Spanish explorer Don Francisco Tapia was commissioned to survey the Florida coast, and in 1693 drew the first known map of East Pass and its shores.

The most recognized figure in the coastal city's history, however, came along much later — Captain Leonard Destin.

A native of New London, Connecticut, Destin settled in Northwest Florida in 1845. He is acknowledged as the pioneer of a fishing port that now holds the largest fleet in North America.

Destin earned its city charter under the laws of the state of Florida in 1984. An interesting note is that the 100 fathom curve draws closer to Destin than any other spot in Florida, providing the fastest deep-water access on the Gulf of Mexico.

CHARTER BOAT
BILLFISHER
COAST GUARD LICENSED UP TO 17 PASS.
CAPT. DAVE GIRARD   PH. 837-2324

FORT WALTON BEACH

Did you know there was never a Fort Walton?

According to exploresouthernhistory.com, Fort Walton Beach traces its name to a Civil War camp established by the Walton Guards in 1861.

The guards, who protected the waters from Destin's East Pass through Choctawhatchee Bay to Santa Rosa Sound, were comprised of men from Walton and Santa Rosa counties. Remember, Okaloosa County did not exist until 1915.

The Walton Guards made camp in the heart of what is now downtown Fort Walton Beach. The outpost was called "Camp Walton." The namesake remains today.

NAVARRE

About forty-one years before Guy H. Wyman platted Navarre, a small settlement named Eagan arose in 1884. The settlement, composed of forty families, was located off the Santa Rosa Sound. It encompassed a portion of present-day Navarre and existed as a post office location.

The interesting part about Wyman, a U.S. Army colonel, is that during World War I, he met a French nurse named Noel. Immigration laws at the time wouldn't allow him to bring her back to the country as his fiancée or wife, but he could bring her back as his legal child.

So Wyman adopted Noel and settled in the Florida Panhandle, where he purchased a large amount of land in 1925. Noel named their holdings Navarre after a province in Spain, located near France.

SOUTH WALTON

Grayton Beach is the focal point for the early development that transformed South Walton County into today's renowned destination site of sixteen beach communities.

In 1890, General William Miller and William Wilson moved their families to the coast and mapped out the village that would become Grayton Beach. Named after Major Charles T. Gray, who built a coastal homestead in 1885, the village celebrates its 126th year of existence in 2016.

During the decade of the 1910s, W.H. Butler and his son, Van, moved from New York to South Walton and bought most of the land in Grayton Beach, which led to the community's first major development.

World War II also played a role in further growth, as the U.S. Coast Guard established a station in Grayton Beach. Over the next decade, beach neighborhoods that now constitute Inlet Beach and Seagrove were established.

From there, a playground for the rich and famous blossomed. The famed 18.5-mile County Road 30A corridor (plus 9.4 miles of connector roads) was completed in the 1970s and earned Scenic Highway designation in the 2000s.

Portions of this snapshot on Emerald Coast history were taken from "Okaloosa County Memories," a special centennial edition published by the Northwest Florida Daily News in 2014.

Recipe Index

Beach Index

Chef Index

Restaurant Index

NORTHWEST FLORIDA
Daily News

Northwest Florida Daily News, owned by GateHouse Media, LLC, has been a local source of vetted news in the area since 1946. As community members of the gorgeous Emerald Coast of Florida for seventy years, our photographers, reporters, and managers know the best the area has to offer and hope to share that knowledge through this stunning collection of images and local recipes, which you can enjoy in your own home.

Additional copies of *Navigate the Emerald Coast*
may be obtained by contacting us at:
Northwest Florida Daily News
2 Eglin Parkway NE.
Fort Walton Beach, FL 32548
800-755-1185
nwfdailynews.com

Publisher: Diane Winnemuller
Editor: Bob Heist
Advertising: Donna Talla
Contributors: Jennie McKeon, Deborah Wheeler, Savannah Vasquez, Nick Tomecek, Devon Ravine, and Michael Snyder

ISBN: 978-0-87197-642-0
Library of Congress Control Number: 2016950006
Printed in China
10 9 8 7 6 5 4 3 2 1

Published by GateHouse Media, LLC

Historic Hospitality Books

Navigate the Emerald Coast was edited, designed, and manufactured by Historic Hospitality Books in collaboration with Northwest Florida Daily News. Historic Hospitality Books creates exquisitely designed custom books for America's iconic hotels, inns, resorts, spas, and historic destinations. Historic Hospitality Books is an imprint of Southwestern Publishing Group, Inc., 2451 Atrium Way, Nashville, Tennessee 37214. Southwestern Publishing Group is a wholly owned subsidiary of Southwestern/Great American, Inc., Nashville, Tennessee.

Christopher G. Capen, President, Southwestern Publishing Group, Inc.
Sheila Thomas, President and Publisher, Historic Hospitality Books
Steve Newman, Cover and Layout Designer
Kristin Connelly, Managing Editor
Linda Brock, Project Manager and Editor

www.swpublishinggroup.com | 800-358-0560